Halfway to para

IT was a decade of smiles and tears. Liverpool,like the rest of the country, was still picking itself up after the terrible cost of the Second World War as the 1950s dawned.

Much of Europe was still in ruins, cities scarred by bomb craters. Rationing didn't end until 1954, many Liverpool streets were still lit by gas, most homes were without any central heating and families gathered round the wireless set for entertainment.

Two million people on Merseyside joined in the fun for the Festival of Britain celebrations in 1951.

It was, said the Liverpool Echo at the time, a "sorely needed tonic" after the war austerity.

By the end of the decade, most Britons were experiencing the sort of lifestyle that later generations regarded as commonplace.

As the 1950s went on, more and more people were able to bring entertainment into their homes through the television and increase their freedom of travel with the car.

If seeing the working classes as part of the consumer culture was new, so was the recognition that teenagers were part of the same market, with money to spend on music and fashion.

Despite the changes, the 1950s still represented conservatism. TV and cinema showed a cosy, moral world where authority was respected and class barriers remained in place.

By the end of the decade, British Prime Minister Harold Macmillan was able to tell the electorate: "You've never had it so good."

He was probably right.

Words and pictures: Vicky Andrews

Photography: Liverpool Daily Post and Echo Archives

Cover design: Zoe Egan

Design/layout: Zoe Egan, Vicky Andrews and Colin Harrison

Published by: Trinity Mirror Merseyside, PO Box 48, Old Hall Street, Liverpool L69 3EB

Printed by: Precision Colour Printing, Telford

ISBN: 978 1 9006802 17 2

Making the News 1950

THE CAMEO MURDER

The Cameo Cinema, Wavertree and below, queues formed every day outside St George's Hall for the murder trial. The last film shown at The Cameo was Calcutta starring Alan Ladd, in January 1957

THE Liverpool Cameo Cinema murder gripped the imagination of Merseyside in 1950, when a young labourer was sent to the gallows.

When two shots rang out in the cinema in Webster Road, Wavertree, on March 19 1949, it was not an imaginary screen drama, but a real life horror story. One man was dead, another died within a few hours.

It was about 9.30pm on that fateful Saturday night when Leonard Thomas, 44, manager of the cinema, and his assistant Bernard Catterall, 30, were shot by a man who burst in with an automatic pistol.

An investigation followed that had all the tension of a gangster movie. About 75,000 people were interviewed, 10,000 houses visited. Police took into possession a shotgun, 30 revolvers and three rifles.

George Kelly and Charles Connolly were charged in October 1949 and tried together at St George's Hall. But after 13 days, the judge ordered separate trials.

Kelly was first to stand trial alone and, despite the prosecution having no forensic evidence, no eyewitnesses and no murder weapon, he was found guilty. He was hanged on March 28, 1950.

Charles Connolly, terrified he, too, would face the death penalty, was persuaded by his lawyer to plead guilty to robbery after a deal was struck with the prosecution.

He died in 1997, still protesting his innocence with the support of his family and his friends.

Eventually, in 2003, it emerged at the Court of Appeal – where the convictions of both Kelly and Connolly were posthumously quashed – that a statement given to detectives by a prosecution witness, claiming a man called Donald Johnson confessed to the crime, had not been disclosed to the defence.

memorable movies!

Clement Attlee

Joe Gibbins, Parliamentary Labour candidate for Liverpool Toxteth, addresses a crowd on a Blitz site at Park Street, February 14, 1950

NATIONAL HEADLINES

24 February: The Labour Party wins the general election, with Clement Attlee returning as Prime Minister. The result is the closest for 100 years.

26 May: Long queues appear at garages and motorists tear up their ration books after the government announces an end to petrol rationing.

25 June: North Korea invades South Korea at several points along the two countries' joint border.

15 August: Princess Anne of Edinburgh is born at Clarence House in London.

29 August: A British force of about 4,000 infantry arrives in Korea from Hong Kong, as back up for the American-led United Nations force.

9 September: Post-war soap rationing ends.

Top of the Pops:

Charts of record sales did not begin in the UK until November 1952, when The Hit Parade was first published by the NME. However, sheet music sales charts pre-1952 show the most popular songs of the time, plus the most notable recordings of the songs that were in the shops.

- Frank Sinatra – Goodnight Irene
- Eve Young & The Homesteaders – (If I Knew You Were Coming) I'd've Baked A Cake
- Teresa Brewer – Music! Music! Music!
- Billy Eckstine – My Foolish Heart
- Bing Crosby – Rudolph the Red Nosed Reindeer

Frank Sinatra

From the blitz to the glitz

Dior's dazzling new look

GLAMOUR arrived as a dramatic change from wartime austerity.

There was a hangover from the war years and people in the early 50s were still having to make do and mend.

For a while after World War II, fashion continued much as it had done during the war, although scandalised older members of society would occasionally spot a girl wearing trousers.

Three years before the Fifties had even begun, Christian Dior's iconic New Look, with its emphasised narrow waists and voluminous skirts had rocked the Paris catwalks.

The sack dress shown by Givenchy at the 1957 Paris collections

Glamour girls – "Does one's posterior look big in this?"

While most Liverpool women were still restricted by financial hardship and limited clothing coupons, they gazed longingly at the image of an elegant screen siren with the perfect figure and clothing reminiscent of the Belle Epoque era of the early 1900s.

The fashionable boutiques that were starting to open in London had still not made it to Liverpool. Women shopped in department stores such as George Henry Lee, Hendersons and Cripps of Bold Street. The older generation favoured places like The Fifty Shilling Tailors in London Road and Church Street, the Bon Marche and Blacklers and C&A Modes.

Many men stuck to the traditional dark suit and trilby hat, which they raised when they met women.

Towards the end of the decade, garments were revolutionised by the arrival of new fabrics, such as Nylon, polyester and acrylic.

A net hat and fur wrap, the height of fashion at the races

Coronation year elegance

A relaxing lunch break with the pigeons in Coronation Gardens in 1958

From teddy bears to Teddy Boys

Youngsters lead the charge for change

AT the start of the decade, the most fashionable age to be was between thirty and forty.

Children dressed like their parents and wore their hair in the same styles and the shops in Liverpool reflected that.

Many young people chose conventional fashions – sharp shirts and jackets for the boys and neat pleated skirts and scoop neck blouses for the girls.

But rock and roll ripped up the songbook and changed the way teenagers dressed. Along came the Beat Generation, in their turtleneck sweaters, berets and dark glasses.

The Teddy Boys, named after the Edwardian-style clothes they wore, had long drape jackets, swept back haircuts, crepe-soled shoes and what would later be known as drainpipe trousers.

Teenage girls gossiped in coffee shops and jived at the Cavern, their circle skirts twirling as they danced.

Everyone wanted a rock or film star's hairstyle – a DA – 'ducks arse', backsweep, a Beachy Head, a bap, bepop, a crest, a dupe, a Panama or a tevee. The Beehive style worn by Dusty Springfield was all the rage among teenage girls with hair rolled into a cone and coated with hairspray.

A 1958 headturner

Young fashion – stepping out in style

This snap of a wistful Fifties girl was taken in L8 by Anne Josephine Hawes

Going places

Reinventing the wheel

THE Liverpool tramway system just before the Second World War was second to none.

But the war was a turning point in the tramway's history. When air raids damaged the tracks or overhead power lines, repairs took some time. Buses, on the other hand, could be back in service very quickly.

Buses gradually replaced the trams and in 1957 the last Baby Grands – four wheelers which operated on more congested routes – were withdrawn from service.

Huge crowds went to the Pier Head to see the last trams set off, closing a colourful chapter in Liverpool's history.

One of the biggest lifestyle changes was the motorcar, which made inroads into bus and train passenger numbers as well as giving ordinary people the chance to explore. Travel until then had been only for the rich. Now people who had been confined to places where public transport could take them, could go where they pleased.

In 1958, the first UK motorway, the M6, opened and a year later the much-loved MINI car put in its first appearance.

The King's Square entrance to the Queensway Mersey Tunnel, taken in spring 1953

Left: Two days until Christmas 1958 and Liverpool's Whitechapel is packed not with shoppers but with cars. Pictured below: Lunchtime by the Mersey, May 1959

End of the line in sight for steam – The Shamrock from Euston pulls into Lime Street, hauled by an English Electric Deltic, December 1955

A procession of Baby Grands on the last day of Liverpool's trams, 14 September, 1957

Liverpool's last tram – now in the Seashore Trolley Museum in Kennebunkport, Maine, USA

A tram passes beneath the Overhead Railway

A crowded carriage on the last day of service for the Liverpool Overhead Railway, 1956

End of the line

Farewell to the wonderful Ovee

LIVERPOOL said goodbye to a dear old friend in 1956, when the Overhead Railway closed.

The 'Ovee' was one of the city's most useful and fascinating features, stretching alongside the docks and river for more than six miles, with 17 stations between Dingle and Seaforth.

Typical Liverpool humour named the railway The Dockers' Umbrella.

It was a railway built ahead of its time and there was a lot of dismay in the city when it was decided to close this remarkable railway.

Although it still carried nearly 10m passengers a year, it was in dire need of repair.

But the cost, around 2m, was beyond the company's means and it was closed on Sunday, December 30, 1956.

Prince's Dock in 1954, showing the Overhead Railway

THE FESTIVAL OF BRITAIN

ON Merseyside an astonishing two million people joined in the fun of the Festival of Britain.

There were processions, concerts, river pageants, exhibitions and firework displays.

Sir Gerald Barry, originator of the idea for holding the Festival, came to see for himself Merseyside's response.

He found that for a city of 790,000 people, there were two million visitors and spectators at the events, despite frequent rainstorms. Sir Gerald pronounced Liverpool's contribution to the celebrations as the best in the country outside London.

The Festival, devised to celebrate the centenary of Prince Albert's Great Exhibition, came at a time when rationing was still in force and some of Liverpool's streets were still lit by gas.

These were the austerity years, but Merseyside put on its happy face and celebrated in style. Liverpool's Festival opened with record crowds and a special service at Liverpool Cathedral, where the Archbishop of York, Dr Cyril Garbett, preached. More than 6,000 heard the service and the congregation overflowed into the aisle and transepts. Many crowded outside.

The streets were jammed with sightseers for the first official event of the Festival – the mounting of the Town Hall guard.

In the afternoon, elephants arrived for the Festival circus and the crowds were said by the Liverpool Echo to resemble those on VE night.

Around 20,000 visitors went on board the six warships on Merseyside for the celebrations and sailors had to help police control crowds at the dock gates where many waited three hours.

More than 50,000 people lined both banks of the Mersey to watch 2,000 rockets released in probably the greatest display of fireworks ever seen in Britain.

The crowds stretched from Seaforth to Garston on the Liverpool side and from New Brighton almost to Ellesmere Port on the other side.

Before the fireworks there was a parade of Mersey's little ships – tugs, dredgers and ferry boats. The celebrations continued throughout July and August.

Merseyside and Youth', one of three major Festival processions in Liverpool in August 1951, passes along Church Street

Liver Bird banners stand proud over the Mersey Tunnel entrance

memorable movies!

The displays on the canopy of C&A Modes look over Church Street. In the background the rebuilding of Lewis's can be seen

NATIONAL HEADLINES

17 April: British submarine The Affray, carrying 75 crew members, goes missing off the south coast of England. 26 ships and submarines from four countries - Britain, France, Belgium and the US - were involved in the search.

3 May: King George opens the Festival of Britain, marking the centenary of the Great Exhibition of 1851.

28 May: Crazy People is first broadcast on the BBC Home Service. It would subsequently be known as The Goon Show.

23 September: Crowds gather outside Buckingham Palace to hear news of King George IV, after an operation to remove part of his lung.

26 October: Winston Churchill wins the general election for the Conservative Party, making him Prime Minister for the second time.

31 October: Zebra crossings are introduced.

20 November: More than 1,000 families of British servicemen begin moving out of the Suez Canal Zone town of Ismailia. Tensions between the British and Egyptians were running high since the government in Cairo stepped up its demands for the complete withdrawal of British troops.

Top of the Pops:

- Mel Blanc – I Taut I Taw A Puddy Tat
- Nat King Cole – Too Young
- Patti Page – The Tennessee Waltz
- Les Paul & Mary Ford – Mockin' Bird Hill
- Mario Lanza – The Loveliest Night Of The Year

Nat King Cole

The smell of fried onions and candy floss, the laughter of the children, donkeys and deck chairs. Unforgettable. A bank holiday evening in 1957

Great escapes

Oh, we do like to be beside the seaside!

SUNSHINE would bring thousands of Liverpool folk to the Pier Head, all eager to enjoy the best of the weather while it lasted.

They headed down to the Mersey en masse to wait for ferryboats to take them on a sunny day trip. Families would spend a holiday strolling on the piers or building sandcastles in Southport, Freshfields and Crosby, or picnics in Formby dunes with Dad burning sausages over a Primus stove. Nothing could beat the fun of a day at New Brighton boating lake for youngsters and adults alike.

A highlight for many was the Miss New Brighton bathing contest, which began in 1949.

In 1950, Violet Pretty became the holder of the title – she would later become known to millions as actress Anne Heywood through her work with The Rank Organisation.

Sunseekers make the most of the summer in St John's Gardens, 1955.
Below: Some Liverpool lads help a party of Swedish girls with their luggage as they arrive for a stay at Colomendy in August 1953

In the 1950s, many of those lucky enough to afford a 'jolly' headed to a holiday camp. Sir Billy Butlin believed in giving value for money, the main ingredient in his phenomenal success.

The jolly atmosphere, camaraderie, top-line dance orchestras and variety shows, beauty contests, glamorous granny competitions, and, yes, even the knobbly knees competitions along with the hi-de-hi's and ho-de-ho's added up to a great week of fun.

Many stars got their first break into stardom while working at the Pwllheli centre in the 50s including Jimmy Tarbuck, Clinton Ford and Michael Holliday.

The car took people to places they had never been before. Holidays abroad also began to take off for the masses in 1950 – Gerard Blitz, a Belgian, started tourist holidays in Majorca, with cheap accommodation in army surplus tents.

A steady stream of 'charas' heading though the tunnel on an overcast August Bank Holiday morning in 1952

Hercules CYCLES
The Finest Bicycle Built Today
BENT'S ALES
ALES BENT'S STOUT
WARDS & Cº
EDWARDS & Cº
BARGAIN CORNER
LLEWELLYNS
ABC
FJF 691
HKF 336

FLYING ENTERPRISE

FLYING Enterprise made international headlines in 1952 when one man battled desperately to save her during one of the worst storms in history.

Flying Enterprise, a C1-type cargo Liberty ship set out from Hamburg to the USA on December 21, 1951, under the command of Kurt Carlsen.

Her official cargo included 1300 tons of pig iron and 900 tons of coffee, plus 10 passengers. Some 400 miles off Land's End on Christmas night, Flying Enterprise hit a storm and after a battering from the sea, developed severe structural damage with a stress crack across her main deck.

An SOS was issued on December 28, by which time The Flying Enterprise was listing precariously to one side.

As the drama unfolded in the Atlantic, America sent destroyers to guard the ship night and day. But what exactly was it carrying, and why were the US Navy so concerned about its sinking?

On December 29 the crew and passengers were evacuated onto a US destroyer – all except Captain Kurt Carlsen, who remained on board for almost two weeks, trying to secure towlines from rescue ships to get The Flying Enterprise to Falmouth in one piece.

But it proved impossible for any ship to take Flying Enterprise in tow.

"Flying Enterprise lost: Captain, Mate safe," was the headline in the Liverpool Echo on Thursday, January 10, 1952.

"One of the great sea dramas of the century came to an end today with the loss of the Flying Enterprise when almost within sight of safety.

"Her Danish captain Kurt Carlsen, whose courageous decision to remain with his ship *"until I am towed or sunk"* won the admiration of the world, and Kenneth Dancy, of Hook Green near Tunbridge Wells, who risked his life when he jumped from the rescue tug Turmoil to join Captain Carlsen, were saved."

Captain Carlsen and his British helper Kenneth Dancy clamber around the rails of their heavily listing home, the sinking Flying Enterprise, for a check on condition

King George VI

memorable movies!

Al Martino

NATIONAL HEADLINES

10 January: Flying Enterprise sinks some 35 miles off the coast of Cornwall, after a failed two-week long rescue mission.

1 February: The first TV detector van, for tracking down users of unlicensed television sets, is unveiled in the UK.

6 February: King George VI dies, aged 56. He is succeeded by his daughter, Princess Elizabeth, Duchess of Edinburgh.

30 April: The moving diary of Anne Frank, a Jewish victim of the Holocaust, is now available in British book shops entitled The Diary of a Young Girl.

2 May: The world's first ever jet airliner, the BOAC Comet G-ALYP, begins its maiden flight from London to Johannesburg.

3 October: News is announced of the end of tea rationing. It means Britons will soon be able to enjoy unlimited "cuppas" for the first time in 12 years.

5 November: General Dwight D Eisenhower sweeps to victory in the American presidential elections.

25 December: Millions of British and Commonwealth listeners tune in to hear Queen Elizabeth's first Christmas broadcast of her reign.

Top of the Pops:

- Guy Mitchell – There's Always Room at Our House
- Nat King Cole – Unforgettable
- Vera Lynn – Auf Wiederseh'n Sweet-heart
- Jo Stafford – A-round the Corner
- Al Martino – Here in my Heart (Britain's first NME Chart number one)

Rock and roll is here to stay

Fever pitch as fans wreck seats

IN the 1950s rock and roll was born. Everyone bought 78rpm records by Elvis Presley, Fats Domino, Little Richard, Buddy Holly, Chuck Berry and the like.

John Lennon once said: "If you tried to give rock 'n' roll another name you might call it Chuck Berry."

Bill Haley recorded Rock Around the Clock, probably the most famous rock and roll song ever. It sold over 15m copies and stayed in the British charts for more than one year.

When Bill Haley and the Comets visited Liverpool Odeon in 1957, the fans reached such a fever pitch that they wrecked 140 seats.

The Merseysippi Jazz Band with Louis Armstrong

Gerry Marsden leads the Red Mountain Skiffle Group in Don't You Rock Me Daddy-o at the Florence Institute on March 18, 1957

Halfway to Paradise – Billy Fury

Legendary singer Buddy Holly played Liverpool's Philharmonic Hall in 1958 during his one and only UK tour. He was supported by The Tanner Sisters, Gary Miller and "the comedian with the modern style," Des O'Connor.

Merseyside's own rock and roller was Billy Fury, who started his career playing venues all over the city. The Garston-born singer became one of the biggest heartthrobs of his era and hit the high notes with his record Halfway to Paradise.

He was born Ronald Wycherley in 1940 and worked as a tugboat hand with the Alexandra Towing Company before getting his big break when he arrived unannounced at the Birkenhead Essoldo.

Impresario Larry Barnes signed him up, put him on stage and renamed him Billy Fury. He had 26 hit records but never had a number one.

On the night of January 16, 1957, some 600 jazz fans packed into the basement of 10 Mathew Street and more were locked out.

That was the opening of The Cavern Club and topping the bill were the Merseysippi Jazz Band, joined by the Coney Island Skiffle Group, the Wall City Jazzmen and the Ralph Watmough Jazz Band.

Holliday by the Mersey

The story of his life

MICHAEL Holliday was born Norman Alexander Milne in Liverpool in 1925.

This affable singer had his own TV series, two number one hits and was regarded as Liverpool's 'Bing Crosby'.

He was born in Kirkdale and went away to sea, winning a talent contest in New York after being egged on to enter by his shipmates.

After winning another contest in Liverpool's Locarno Ballroom he took up full time singing with bands and in 1955 he turned solo and signed a record deal.

His very first release, Yellow Rose of Texas was a hit and more followed including Story of my Life and Starry Eyed.

Dog-tired but proud of her roots

Liverpool's first chart-topper

ALTHOUGH melancholic passionate ballads were her forte, it was How Much is That Doggy in the Window? that saw Lita Roza become the first female singer to hit the number one spot in the British record charts.

The only problem was that she hated the song, a twee children's singalong which had been a Stateside hit for Patti Page.

Lita was one of seven children born in Upper Pitt Street in Toxteth.

She eventually joined a big band and was named as Britain's top girl singer for five years from 1951 to 1955.

Frankie in it for kicks

Too Marvellous For Words

ENTERTAINER Frankie Vaughan was that most rare of individuals – a showbusiness superstar and a man of the people.

Born Frank Ephraim Abelson in Devon Street, off London Road, Liverpool, on February 3, 1928, he loved his home city with a passion.

He was the bridge between music-hall and rock and roll, twirling his cane with the best of them, while crooning for the moonlight and quickening lonely hearts.

Frankie Vaughan was dedicated to fashion, with his perfectly tailored suits, shining shoes, the cane and boater.

His hits during the 50s included Istanbul, Green Door and Garden of Eden. He also made a number of film appearances including, most notably, in 1960, Let's Make Love starring Marilyn Monroe.

SHOCK WAVES AROUND THE WORLD

THE destruction of the Canadian Pacific liner Empress of Canada by fire in Gladstone Dock on January 25, 1953, made world headlines.

More than 200 firemen from two counties fought the blaze for days to save her – but without success. She heeled over and became a charred hulk.

Raising her proved a great salvage feat and she was towed away for scrap in September, 1954. The cause of the fire was probably a discarded cigarette end.

The ship had been undergoing her Coronation year overhaul and had been towed the previous day from the graving dock to Gladstone number one basin.

Firemen, almost hidden in the steam and smoke, took up perilous positions on the starboard side of the ship, watched by hundreds of dockers waiting for work.

The new cargo shed was badly damaged when the Empress fell against it, her masts and two funnels striking it with force, tearing away stone and cement work.

The masts and funnels were dislodged from their foundations and with the ship lying on her side, stood perpendicular.

For more than six hours 200 firemen from Bootle, Liverpoool, Birkenhead, Lancashire and Cheshire attacked the flames.

By a cruel stroke of fate, Liverpool's fireboat William Gregson was in dock undergoing her first overhaul for 19 months and could not help.

The fire was discovered at 4.15pm on the Sunday, when smoke was seen coming from the ship's dispensary by workmen.

The fire got hold between decks and within two hours had spread the whole width of the ship. Attempts by the Mersey Docks and Harbour Board salvage ship Salvor to flood the lower holds to correct the list, now 16 degrees, were abandoned. By 9.45pm all firemen were withdrawn from the ship and the firefighting continued from the quayside.

At 2.10am a Canadian Pacific Company spokesman said the ship was a total loss.

The Empress of Canada as she was gradually raised in March 1954

The Empress begins her last journey from the Mersey

Royal celebration:
The Coronation of Queen Elizabeth II

Edmund Hillary conquers mighty Mount Everest

memorable movies!

Frankie Laine

NATIONAL HEADLINES

25 January: Canadian Pacific liner Empress of Canada is destroyed by fire.

5 March: Joseph Stalin, the long-time leader of the Soviet Union, dies following a long illness.

24 March: Queen Mary, the Queen's grandmother, dies peacefully in her sleep, aged 85.

13 April: Ian Fleming publishes his first James Bond novel, Casino Royale, in the UK.

25 April: Watson and Crick publish their findings on the double helix structure of a chemical called deoxyribonucleic acid, or DNA.

29 May: Edmund Hillary conquers Everest, the highest peak in the world.

2 June: Queen Elizabeth II is crowned at a coronation ceremony in Westminster Abbey in London.

27 July: The United States, North Korea and China sign an armistice to end The Korean War.

26 November: Peers in the House of Lords back the Conservative Government's proposals for the introduction of commercial television - despite fierce opposition from some rebels.

Top of the Pops

- Perry Como – Don't Let The Stars Get In Your Eyes
- Guy Mitchell – Look At That Girl
- The Stargazers – Broken Wings
- Lita Roza – How Much is That Doggie In The Window
- Frankie Laine – Answer Me

The Palladium, West Derby Road, closed in 1956 after giving 50 years of pleasure to Scouse filmgoers

Stars of the silver screen

An epic love story

SOME called them flea-pits, but on Saturday nights they were palaces.

The boy in the foyer, with his chin shaved pink, was a prince waiting for his princess to step off the bus and walk towards him across the mossy, crimson carpet, so that they could spend a night of romance on the back-seats, under the smoke plumes, while the action danced across the big white screen.

Cinemas were the great escape of the 20th century, when the gods and goddesses were lights and shadows on celluloid.

There were Empires, Roxys, Regals, Plazas, Forums, Trocaderos, Hippodromes, Royals, Ritzes, Scalas, Rialtos, Gaumonts, Regents, Rios and Reos, Palladiums and Olympias.

There will never be another time like it. The stars then were truly great and going to the cinema brought romance and colour into every day life. Many people went twice a week and more.

In 1954 the Odeon on London Road became Liverpool's first large-screen Cinemascope cinema. The Robe, was the first to be shown on the new big curved screen.

Hollywood stars like Gregory Peck and Margaret Lockwood, seen here at the Ritz in Birkenhead, were frequent visitors to Merseyside cinemas in the Fifties

Stanley Baker, star of Violent Playground, meets some of the children of the Liverpool streets. Right, The Magnet directed by Charles Frend

Matinee fun

The ABC Minors

THE Saturday matinee really was the treat of the week for a child of the Fifties.

Waiting noisily for the doors to open at 11am, discussing with your mates how the hero could possibly get out of last week's predicament in the serial, though you knew he would, after all there were still eight chapters to go.

You settled in through Pathé News, the cartoon, the short and the serial – Flash Gordon and Batman & Robin were some of our favourites. We proudly wore our badges and sucked on gobstoppers that lasted the whole performance.

Sometimes the manager would stop the film and told everyone to behave, or else he'd cancel the films and send us off home. Of course, he never did.

Basil Dearden, director of Violent Playground, with Anne Heywood

Lights, camera... action!

Mersey's starring role

BRIGHTON sounds the quintessential seaside location for an Ealing Studios film, but what about New Brighton?

The resort became the setting for the 1950 Ealing Studios adventure film The Magnet, starring the young William Fox.

The Magnet was shot on location in New Brighton, Wallasey, Birkenhead, Liverpool 8 and the Pier Head.

Liverpool really is the world in one city – which is why film crews worldwide have always flocked to use our streets and buildings.

Some of Frankie Vaughan's first film, These Dangerous Years (1957), was set on the Cast Iron shore, Dingle, which he had visited with his grandmother.

In 1958 Liverpool and rock took a knock in Violent Playground.

Based on the novel by James Kennaway, Violent Playground tells of a policeman (Stanley Baker), who is asked to track down a fireraiser (the young David McCallum) in a tough neighbourhood, where Peter Cushing is the parish priest.

Dramas from the north were in vogue in the late 1950s, the time of the Angry Young Men. But the film's climax would have been gripping in any age.

The backdrop for the film was Gerard Gardens and the experts in London said it was "a slice of social realism."

In fact it was so 'real' that the men behind the cameras brought a bundle of ragged, grey washing to hang on the lines, so that the people would look poorer.

DO NOT
FEED
THE

Arthur Askey greets Frankie Vaughan in the 1956 film 'Ramsbottom Rides Again'. The classic British Fifties cast included Sabrina, Sid James, Jerry Desmonde and Shani Wallis

Above: Wallasey-born Brian Reece played Police Constable Archibald Berkeley-Willoughby known as PC 49 in the popular radio series of the Forties and Fifties, The Adventures of PC 49

Two of Liverpool's comedy greats, Derek Guyler and Robb Wilton

SCALA

Entertainment for the people

Circus spectacular tops the bill

WHEN Billy Smart's Circus paraded through Liverpool in 1959, complete with costumed elephants, the streets were packed.

An immense crowd of thousands brought traffic in Lime Street to a complete halt. The throng extended in one continuous carpet from Renshaw Street, beyond the Adelphi Hotel to the far side of St George's Plateau. As the parade moved on, the crowds extended to Leece Street and right out of town to Sefton Park.

The procession came at the end of a long and hot summer but organisers said that even on a rainy day they would have expected much the same response.

The glitter and colour was particularly attractive to the hundreds of children who provided a front-row apron to the cavalcade.

Hopalong Cassidy (William Boyd) on a visit to the American Airbase at Burtonwood in 1954

Above: Billy Martins Modern and Latin formation teams appeared on Victor Sylvester's Come Dancing show in 1959

Liverpool Corporation Passenger Transport Band in Coronation Gardens in 1959

Vernons Girls

Pools ensemble make television splash

THE Vernons Girls (pictured left) emerged from the Liverpool pools company and appeared in all 38 editions of the television show Oh Boy!

Jack Good, the pop mogul, booked an array of international stars for Oh Boy! on ITV.

Central to it all were the Vernons Girls, who by then were being recruited from beyond the pools company. The girls made an Oh Boy! album with Cliff, the John Barry Seven, Cuddly Dudley, Peter Elliott, and Neville Taylor and the Cutters.

MP Bessie Braddock shows Russian delegates the sights of Liverpool, July 24, 1956

Battling Bessie

Queen of politics

BESSIE Braddock – a true heroine of the 20th century – was the embodiment of the militant Liverpool housewife in Parliament in the 1950s.

An MP for the Liverpool Exchange Division for 24 years, she became a world personality because of her fiery speeches and battles for the underdog.

Over the years she became one of Parliament's best-known characters, on one occasion in the house Quentin Hogg referred to her as his "pin-up girl". Politics were in her blood. Born in the last year of the 19th century in Zante Street, Liverpool, she went to her first political meeting when three weeks old, carried in her mother's shawl.

She married John Braddock in 1922 and the couple devoted their political energies to the Labour party. John became a councillor for Everton in 1929 and the following year Bessie was returned for St Anne's Ward.

Bessie became a city magistrate the year after being returned as an MP.

Ted Ray

Wit of the wireless

TED Ray was actually born Charlie Ogden in Wigan, but arrived in Liverpool when only a few weeks old in 1909.

He was a natural performer whether playing the halls as 'Nedlo the Gypsy' or presenting Ray's A Laugh and Spot The Tune.

Tommy Steele and Carole Lesley entertain the crowds in Red Square at the 1959 Moscow Film Festival

Tommy Steele

An adopted son

TOMMY Steele was this country's first home produced rock and roll star.

For the Bermondsey-born lad, Liverpool was the city where he had his first job in the Merchant Navy, sailing out of the Mersey for overseas adventures.

In 1956, the year of his first hit, Rock With the Caveman, he rolled up at Liverpool's Royal Court Theatre to appear in his first pantomime, Goldilocks and the Three Bears. Tommy was just 19 and had arrived as a pop singer.

Nicholas Monsarrat on a return visit to Liverpool in 1955

Nicholas Monsarrat

New chapter for Naval memories

NICHOLAS Monsarrat, born John Turney in Liverpool in 1910, wrote the best-selling novel The Cruel Sea, based on his experiences serving in the Navy during World War II. The book came out in 1951 and was filmed in 1953.

Monsarrat, who studied at Cambridge and abandoned law for literature, repeated that success with The Story of Esther Costello in 1953.

He settled in Ottawa, Canada, as director of the UK Information Office. He died in 1979.

Making the News

1954

THE FOUR-MINUTE MILE

World first: Roger Bannister breaks the four-minute mile

IN May 1954, English athlete Roger Bannister wrote his name into the record books by becoming the first man in history to run a mile under 4 minutes.

The 25-year-old clocked 3 minutes and 59.4 seconds at the Iffley Road track in Oxford watched by around 3,000 spectators.

Bannister was running for the Amateur Athletics Association against his old university in a race carefully planned and orchestrated by two pacemakers: Chris Brasher and Chris Chataway.

He had prepared for the race the previous week at Paddington Green in London in high winds, which no doubt helped as his record breaking run was in gusts of up to 25mph.

Below: The scene at the reopening of the Liverpool Cotton Market, restoring the Futures market to free bidding

memorable movies!

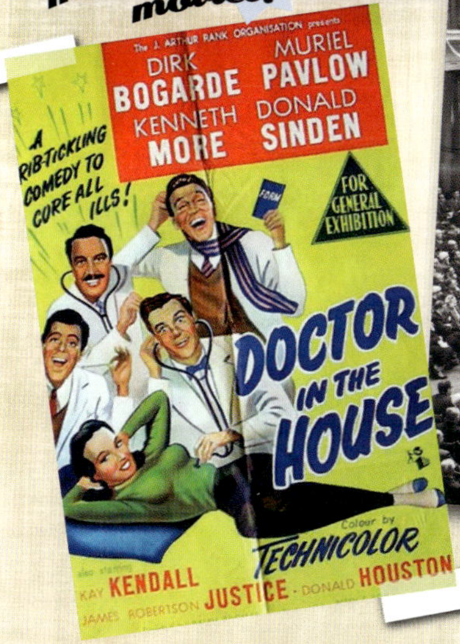

NATIONAL HEADLINES

6 May: Roger Bannister becomes the first man in history to run a mile in under four minutes.

18 May: A new era in the long history of the Liverpool cotton trade is signalled by the ringing of a hand bell on the floor of the Liverpool Cotton Exchange, to mark the reopening of the market after the war.

30 June: Millions of people witness a total eclipse of the sun as the moon cast its shadow from America through Europe and on to Asia.

4 July: Fourteen years of food rationing in Britain ends when restrictions on the sale and purchase of meat and bacon are lifted.

5 July: The BBC broadcasts its first daily television news programme, read by Richard Baker, and replacing the existing Television Newsreel.

4 August: Maiden flight of the English Electric Lightning P1 supersonic jet fighter.

19 October: Britain agrees to end its military occupation of the Suez Canal.

30 November: The Prime Minister, Sir Winston Churchill, celebrates his 80th birthday in a day of ceremonies and tributes to his remarkable career.

Top of the Pops:

- Eddie Calvert – Oh Mein Papa
- Doris Day – Secret Love
- Vera Lynn – My Son My Son
- David Whitfield With Chorus And Mantovani And His Orchestra – Cara Mia
- Winifred Atwell – Let's Have Another Party

Vera Lynn

Notebook, pencil and a few pals. All you needed for trainspotting in 1955

School days great days

Chasing our dreams

'ROLL on four o'clock' was a popular chant back in the 50s as schoolkids progressed from sublime primary to scary secondary modern, while the gifted 11 plussers went on to grammar or technical college.

But we all started out equal. All of us from the class swot to Teddy Boy rebel. We all hated PE and 50s homework BC style (before computers) as well as the visits from the nit nurse and even then redundant careers officer.

We had Colomendy – that summer haven in North Wales to escape to.

Friendships were made sharing sketches from The Goon's radio show.

You played ollies in the jigger and put down coats as posts in the park. "I baggsy being in goal."

Some kids dreamt of never having proper jobs such as Quarry Bank old boy John Lennon and Paul McCartney of the Liverpool Institute and a young George Harrison (smoking behind the bike sheds). In Dingle, Richard Starkey sagged off (played truant). Whatever happened to those four Scouse strangers?

Pupils such as Alan Bleasdale and Willy Russell would even go back to school one day voluntarily . . . as teachers. Crikey!

The best years of our lives indeed – the photos prove it from trips to Chester Zoo and sports days.

What about the teachers? Some funny, some cruel but many were inspirational – they helped us get ready for the outside world.

Just as we helped them . . . in the Liverpool of the 50s.

Home from school, a sugar butty and straight out to play with your mates in the street

Right: Wrapped up well against the rigours of the English summer. New Brighton Model Boating Lake in 1954

Below right: Freezing cold salt water that nearly choked you. It must be Conwallis Street baths

Below left: Wallasey schoolchildren get road safety instruction from the police as the borough's first 'lollipop man' is unveiled in January 1954

The cast iron Bucking Bronco, along with the swings, witch's hat, Maypole and monkey ladder was one of the staples of the Fifties playground

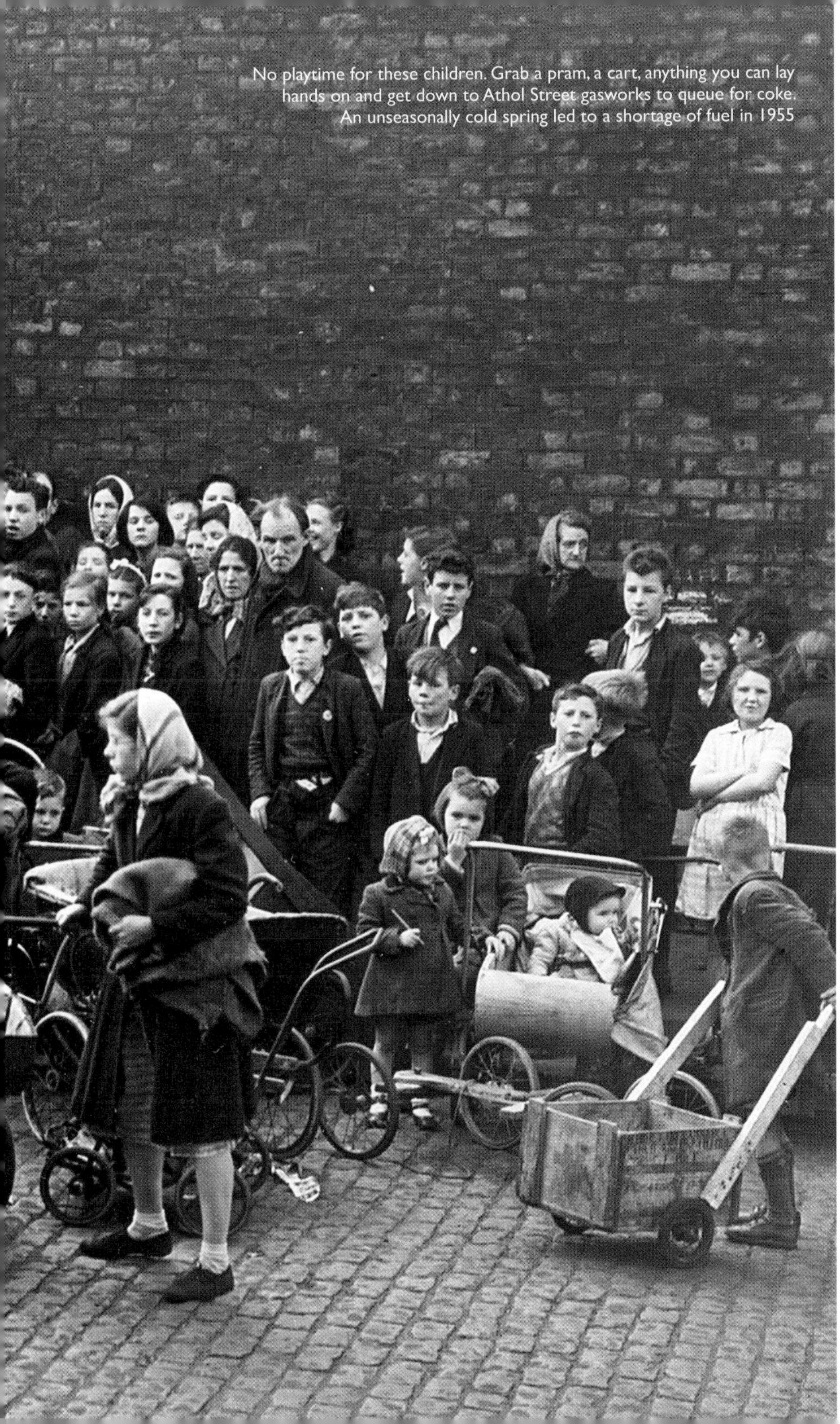

No playtime for these children. Grab a pram, a cart, anything you can lay hands on and get down to Athol Street gasworks to queue for coke. An unseasonally cold spring led to a shortage of fuel in 1955

Scouts from West Derby doing 'bob a job', planting potatoes at Home Farm, Croxteth Park

Daredevils dodging the high tide waves at Egremont in 1950

8 pence a quarter, such a small price to pay for a taste of heaven

Sweet dreams

Sugar rush for treats back on the shelf

ON 5 February 1953 children all over Britain emptied out their piggy-banks and heading straight for the nearest sweet-shop as the first unrationed sweets went on sale.

Wartime restrictions on sweet supplies that had dragged on and on were over.

Toffee apples, sticks of nougat and liquorice strips were snatched up, while some factories gave out free lollipops and sweets. Adults joined in the sugar frenzy, queuing up to buy boiled sweets and boxes of chocolates to take home for the weekend.

Minister of Food, Major Gwilym Lloyd-George, ordered a one-off allocation of extra sugar to manufacturers to help them meet the extra demand. Sugar itself remained rationed until September 1953.

A quarter of sherbert jabs, a bar of five-boys chocolate, two ounces of fruit bowl or a family-size half pound of Trebor's traditional mixture – names to take you back in time.

Remember looking in all the toy shops and comic and sweet shops, stopping for a 1d vantas pulled by a handle from a huge orb-shaped bowl that bubbled and fizzed?

The wondrous smell of pear drops, barley sugar sticks, coconut chips, jap dessert, gobstoppers, lime and soda, bullseyes, banana and custard, love hearts, flying saucers, sweet tobacco and some chewy. A taste of heaven.

Where Eagle dares

Southport's number one space hero

IN post-war Britain, when most children's publications were in black and white, Eagle burst onto the scene with the colourful intergalactic adventures of Dan Dare – Pilot of the Future.

Young readers could let their imaginations run wild as heroic Dan battled his evil arch-nemesis the Mekon in space.

The Eagle was the creation of the Reverend Marcus Morris, then vicar of St James' church, Southport. The Eagle and its sister papers Girl, Swift and Robin were designed by renowned typographer Ruari McLean, and were read by millions throughout the 1950s and 1960s.

The adventures of Dan Dare, created by the genius that was Frank Hampson, rocketed the Eagle to become the most popular comic in British history.

Besides being way ahead of its time artistically, Eagle was also innovative in merchandising for its characters, including ray guns and the Dan Dare Radio Station.

Toys for boys

Hornby treasures for young and old

MECCANO... Hornby... Dinky Toys.

The very mention of these names brings waves of nostalgia flooding back to grown ups – all kids at heart who smile when we hear them.

Dinky toys have been played with by countless thousands of small children – and plenty of big ones too.

The Meccano factory in Binns Road, Liverpool, was a mecca for afficionados of Frank Hornby's famous construction toy. Boys – and occasionally girls – from all corners of the Empire would bombard Meccano HQ with queries and new ideas for products, their enthusiasm fostered by the popular Meccano magazine.

Budding inventors loved making scaled-down models of fire engines and rescue vehicles. Others simply looked at the intricate Dinky models as art forms and were starstruck by Hornby's paintwork: mini-model masterpieces.

Hornby also gave his name to a model railway system and was a gifted inventor. There was a boom period in the 1950s when Meccano would match new vehicles on the roads with toy versions almost as soon as they were launched. Sadly, the famous factory closed in 1979, but the legacy lives on.

Simpler times

Biggest toy was our imagination

THERE is something about the simplicity of 50s childhood that just makes us smile.

We played seasonal games out in the street, with tops and whips, or with a couple of tennis balls against someone's wall. Hide and Seek, Queenie Eye or Kick the Can, with no cars to worry about. Remember Stuck in the Mud, Kingy, or What's the Time Mister Wolf?

Fivestones, jacks, marbles, hopskotch, hula hoops or skipping ropes depending on the current craze.

We had toy soldiers, tin cars, teddy bears, yo-yos, maybe a bicycle if you were really lucky.

Board games were popular too – Ludo, Subbuteo or Snakes and Ladders if it was raining outside. Or the amazing Magic Robot who seemed to know all the answers...

JAMES DEAN'S LAST RIDE

HOLLYWOOD film icon James Dean was killed in a road accident in California, USA on September 30, 1955.

The 24-year-old actor was behind the wheel of his Porsche sports car when it was involved in a head-on collision with another car 30 miles east of Paso Robles.

Dean's mechanic, Rolph Wutherich, who was a passenger in the car, was taken to hospital with serious injuries.

At the time of the accident, the actor – who was a racing enthusiast – was on his way to a race meeting at Salinas in California.

The Liverpool Echo reported on October 1, 1955: "James Dean, 24-years-old film actor, killed in a motoring accident on Friday night, was given a summons for speeding less than two hours before he died, State Police here reported.

"Dean's German Porsche sports car was travelling at 65 miles an hour when police stopped him.

"Officers said that after he received the summons he must have travelled an average speed of nearly 75 miles an hour.

"They made the estimate after checking the time of the summons with that of the fatal accident many miles to the north."

Dean had completed his latest film Giant, an adaptation of Edna Ferber's book about Texas, just the day before the accident.

Dean with his mechanic Rolf Wutherich and friend, preparing his Porsche 550 Spyder for a race

Medics carry the body of James Dean across Highway 466

memorable movies!

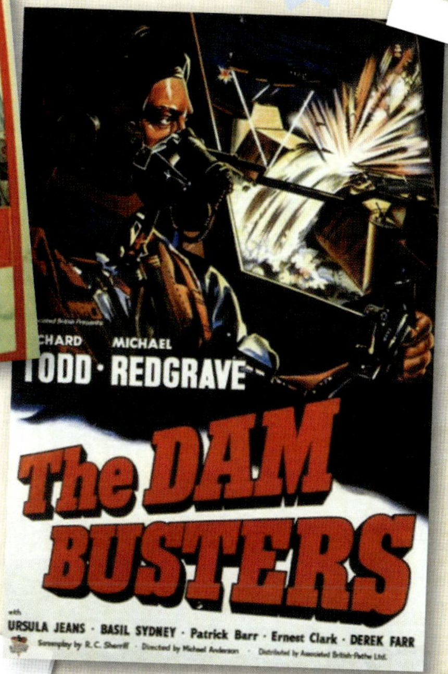

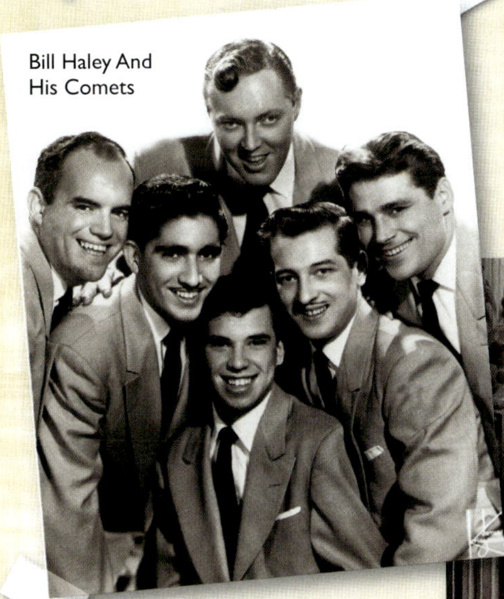
Bill Haley And His Comets

Winston Churchill shakes hands with Sir Anthony Eden on the steps of Downing Street

NATIONAL HEADLINES

24 February: Deep snow and freezing temperatures continue in Britain's big freeze, leaving many parts of the country cut off from essential supplies.

5 April: Sir Winston Churchill resigns as prime minister of Britain due to his failing health. The 80-year-old premier is replaced by Sir Anthony Eden.

9 May: West Germany formally joins the North Atlantic Treaty Organisation.

27 May: The Conservatives win the general election with a clear majority, ending a five-year political stalemate.

13 July: Convicted murderer Ruth Ellis is hanged at Holloway Prison, London. Ellis was sentenced to death at the Old Bailey for shooting her lover, 25-year-old racing driver David Blakely, outside the Magdala public house in London on Easter Sunday.

30 September: James Dean is killed in a road accident, aged 24.

1 December: Mrs Rosa Parks is arrested by police in Montgomery, Alabama, after refusing to give up her seat on the bus to a white person. Segregation laws stated that black Americans must vacate their seats if there are white passengers left standing. Mrs Parks was a youth leader of the local branch of the National Association for the Advancement of Coloured People.

Top of the Pops:

- Slim Whitman – Rose Marie
- Rosemary Clooney – Mambo Italiano
- Tenessee Ernie Ford – Give Me Your Word
- Bill Haley And His Comets – Rock Around The Clock
- Dickie Valentine – Christmas Alphabet

Rodney Street, Birkenhead

Coronation streets

Happy and glorious celebrations

THE rain on Coronation Day didn't dampen the spirits of Merseysiders who celebrated joyfully.

Street parties were the order of the day and for weeks neighbours prepared to stage a glorious party.

Flamboyant decorations and bunting spanned grey terraced streets and houses vied with each other in their colourful crepe, floral facades.

Children wore red, white and blue hats and pumps with paper bows. The pubs were open before breakfast and patriotic songs sung. Some streets crowned their own queen, others made cake replicas of the Queen.

Parents who had worked all day to hold parties for the children found the energy at night to sing and dance in Liverpool's cobbled streets.

Doorsteps were well scrubbed and some pavement

Community spirit, all too soon to be fractured and cast to the Mersey breeze. Danby Street (left) and Abbot Street, both off Heyworth Street, Everton, long fallen beneath the bulldozer

edges were painted in red and white. Dingle looked dazzling, streets in Walton, Wavertree and Scotland Road rustled with loads of streamers and trimmings.

Liverpool Corporation decorations were bathed in floodlights each night and the citizens added coloured bulbs, extra lamps and bonfires to their usual gaslight and electric light.

There was a party for 100 children from Vine Street and Oxford Street in the city centre and another big bash for kids in Barclay Street, Dingle.

Most of Liverpool's churches were filled for Communion services and early morning buses and trams were packed with people travelling to and from church and later to the homes of relatives and friends for television parties.

Coachloads of cheering children waving flags and singing swept through Liverpool all day long.

A Royal Salute was fired by the guns of HMS Sheffield at Gladstone Dock. Just before 9.30pm, more than 200 ships berthed in Merseyside's docks, at a signal given by Sheffield, according to the Liverpool Echo, "let forth their famous cock-a-doodle-dos, part of a round-the-world broadcast of Coronation celebrations."

Outspan oranges for Coronation kids – a rare treat

Subeditors on the old Liverpool Daily Post & Echo offices in Victoria Street, 1950

Clocking on

Good news on the jobs front

DURING wartime, women had been out in the work force to fill the jobs of the men who were off to war.

But now the men were back home and husbands went out to provide for their families.

Traditional roles like the milkman, breadman and coal man were still respectable and if you were really smart and had a way with words, a career at the local newspaper or bank could be on the cards.

The post-war economic boom saw new investment and job opportunities springing up everywhere.

Construction, agriculture, food processing and manufacturing firms flourished, especially those making consumer goods like washing machines and radios. White collar jobs were on the up too and the resulting office growth increased demand for women to work in secretarial, receptionist and support work.

The ladies of the packing and wrapping room at Cadbury's factory in Moreton, September 1954

WRAC recruiting office, Pownall Square, Liverpool, 1959

Fresh to your door. The breadman on his rounds in 1952

Men of the King's Regiment take a break before boarding the troopship Devonshire for Korea

Liverpool's first permanent zebra crossing, laid on Castle Street in front of the Town Hall in 1951

The last working horse delivery milkman on his city centre rounds

Waves of expectation

Docklands were a gateway to the new world

BACK in the 1950s Liverpool did not have to prove it was European – or even world – capital of anything.

The four corners of the earth arrived in freighters through its front door across the Mersey Bar.

Many Liverpool secondary schools offered their pupils an option of learning Spanish.

This was so they could work on the Pacific Steam Navigation Company's ships to the Caribbean, through the Panama Canal and along eastern South America.

Or they could join Booth Line, which sailed 1,000 miles up the Amazon. Or Blue Star Line, the Vestey family's own steamship company, that operated refrigerated ships carrying meat from its vast Argentinian ranch interests.

The post-war years saw the consolidation of the trading routes as Britain settled back into its traditional role as manufacturer to the world.

Prior to containerisation, the docks were big enough to accommodate the post-war typically-sized cargo ships of around 5,000 tons. These were still good times for the Liverpool shipowners.

There were the big glamorous ocean liner companies, such as Anchor, Bibby, Cunard, Canadian Pacific, Elder Dempster and Pacific Steam Navigation. Then there were the equally-famous Liverpool lines which concentrated on cargo liner services, but also carried passengers such as Blue Funnel, Blue Star, Booth, Brocklebank, Clan, Ellerman City & Hall, Harrison, Lamport & Holt, Port Line, Royal Mail and Shaw Savill & Albion.

Between them all, they just about had the world covered.

At this period, all British ships were built in UK shipyards. Cammell Laird at Birkenhead had an enviable reputation building warships, with the aircraft carrier HMS Ark Royal (IV) launched in May 1950 being its most famous post-war Royal Navy ship.

Mention must be made of the last White Star liner, m/v Britannic, which by the 1950s was under Cunard control following the two companies' merger in 1934.

By the end of the 1950s, Cammell Laird had the prestigious contract to build the ultimate South African mail ship, RMS Windsor Castle, launched by the Queen Mother in 1959.

The view from Tranmere Hill in Birkenhead as HMS Ark Royal prepares for launching at Cammell Laird in 1950

John Ross Campbell, editor of the Daily Worker, calls for a show of hands at a meeting of striking dockers at Anfield in 1950

There were still hundreds of horses working on the Docks in the Fifties

Workers in a tobacco warehouse weigh the imported leaves for taxation purposes in 1950

Far left: the 22,000 ton Cunard liner Ivernia, sister ship of Saxonia, In Canada Dock, 19 July 1955

Left: the majestic Empress of England glides past the Whitsuntide holidaymakers at New Brighton

Below: not a container in sight – goods of all shapes and sizes loaded onto rail wagons by hand

Above: Smoke from the chimneys of Clarence Dock Power Station drift across the river in 1957. Princes Dock is sandwiched between the bulk of Riverside Station and the Overhead Railway

Left: The Windsor Castle built at Cammell Laird. Launched in 1959, the largest liner built in England

Far left: The late October sunshine in 1952 turns the Mersey to silver as the Cunard liner Ascania arrives home after another Atlantic crossing

Making the News 1956

THE SUEZ CRISIS

LIVERPOOL DAILY POST

ALLIED PLANES BOMB EGYPT

Military targets only, Selwyn Lloyd tells House of Commons

ALLIES CONDEMNED, BUT—

America will not intervene, says Eisenhower

LABOUR DECLARE WAR ON EDEN

Censure motion to-day

7 a.m.

SUEZ CRISIS

Premier to speak on amendment

United Nations to call General Assembly

CAIRO REPORTS OF RAID ON CAPITAL QUITE UNTRUE

Getting Engaged?

SIR Anthony Eden was in charge during one of Britain's darker moments of the decade, the Suez Crisis.

Eden's decision to support aggression against President Nasser over Egypt's nationalisation of the Suez canal led to international censure and effectively ended his premiership.

The war was a debacle which led to the resignation of the Prime Minister, broken in spirit and health.

Nasser emerged as a champion of Arab unity and was officially elected president in 1956.

Petrol rationing began on December 17, 1956, with fuel shortages throughout Europe. Panic buying caused havoc around the country. Petrol rationing finally ended on 14 May 1957.

Left: The launch of Premium Bonds

Right: Cigarette adverts encouraged smoking before the harmful effects were properly understood

memorable movies!

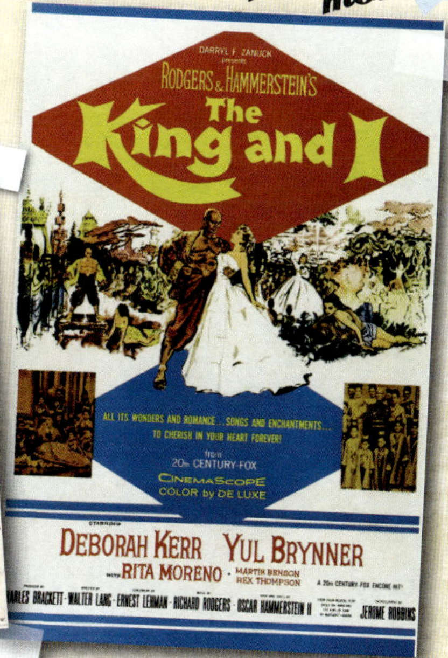

NATIONAL HEADLINES

22 March: Civil rights leader, the Reverend Martin Luther King, is convicted of organising an illegal boycott by black passengers of buses in the US state of Alabama.

17 April: Chancellor of the Exchequer Harold Macmillan introduces Premium Bonds.

3 May: Granada Television launched.

7 May: The Health Minister, RH Turton, rejects calls for a government campaign against smoking, saying no ill-effects have actually been proven.

17 October: The Queen opens the world's first commercial nuclear power station at Calder Hall.

7 November: General Dwight D Eisenhower is returned to the White House with the biggest Republican win since Abraham Lincoln's in 1860.

22 November: Great Britain and Northern Ireland compete at the 1956 Summer Olympics in Melbourne, Australia, and win 6 gold, 7 silver and 11 bronze medals.

23 December: Crowds of Egyptians pour onto the streets of Port Said to celebrate the withdrawal of British and French forces from Egyptian soil.

Top of the Pops:

- Dean Martin – Memories Are Made Of This
- Ronnie Hilton – No Other Love
- The Teenagers – Why Do Fools Fall In Love
- Doris Day – Whatever Will Be Will Be
- Johnnie Ray – Just Walkin In The Rain

The best buys
More for your money

THE 1950s was a time of exciting new trends on the shopping front.

Cars and televisions were the big buys and changed people's lives. And teenagers were born, a new generation of young people who had money to spend and who inspired a new craze in advertising. In 1959 the average male teenager took home £8 a week and the average girl £6 a week. In the early 1950s only privileged people could afford to pay £80 for a TV and in 1953 fewer than two million homes had one. But by 1957 – when the combined radio and TV licence was £4 – more than half the homes in Britain had TV sets.

Adverts of the time show how our ideas about health have changed. A box of cereal selling at 10d or 1s 7d in 1950 boasted in contained 'double sugar' and also extra salt.

Lewis's in Liverpool city centre offered lots of bargains in the sales, including coats at 49s 6d, women's tailored suits at 59s 6d and frocks at 15s. It was a time when women wore hats, nylon blouses, gabardine raincoats, winter overcoats and winceyette pyjamas.

Castle Street in 1954 had all the small shops you could need. A tobacconist, a fruiterers, a tailors, a laundry, an optician, a wine merchant, an art gallery, a booksellers and a cafe can all be seen on this picture

The January sales in full flow in Liverpool in 1957

Women were rushing to C&A in 1950 to buy the new rayon print frocks from as little as 55s, described as "distinctive styles for dressy occasions." They squeezed themselves into girdles like Playtex 'living girdle', the 'magic controller' and the 'trimline girdle'.

Furniture was dull but solid; you could buy walnut suites at just under £60, moquette three-piece suites were around £30, dining room suites in polished oak shade £30, oak bedroom suites with wardrobe, chest of drawers and dressing table £40 and fireside chairs £6 each. Rushworths were selling pianos from £59.

We bought household goods like dish drainers (9s 11d), chromium plated teapots (4s 11d) and rayon taffeta bedspreads (27s 6d). And women were washing up the dishes with the new Quix concentrated suds, just 1s 6d a bottle.

Of course, rationing didn't end until 1954 and the Liverpool Echo published information on where people could get their new ration books.

In 1954 a new Morris Minor cost £439.10s, a new Ford Zephr around £900. Cheap rail fares in the early 1950s from Liverpool Lime Street included Birmingham (10s 6d), Leeds (7s 6d), London (25s), Colwyn Bay (7s 6d) and York (11s 6d).

Shoppers throng Church Street in November 1959. Woolworths, C&A and Coopers can be seen in the background

Bold Street, home of Liverpool's posh shops like Austin Reed, Waring & Gillow, Ciro Pearls and Weatherall Bond Street Ltd

Clockwise from left: Bargains galore in Woolies, Liscard, Wallasey in 1959; Beaver Radio in Whitechapel in 1957; Festival decorations in St John's market, 1951; Coronation decorations in Church Street

The good life

Bringing home the bacon

THERE are certain things in life that you never forget – like your family's Co-op number.

Mother made out the shopping list and it was off with your divi number, first to the bacon counter, then the dry goods and so on. The money was put into a small metal container with the price ticket and sent by overhead wires to the cashier, who sent it back to the assistant with your change.

It was a time when self-service shopping was a novelty and frozen food a wonder.

There was no central heating in homes so people bought electric fires from 15 shillings and oil convectors at just under £5 from Blacklers.

The weekend meant bath night – boiling water to fill up the tin bath in front of the fire and the whole family taking turns to get washed.

The production of sensible but dull Utility Furniture ended in 1952, although the homes of many still featured a set of Cotswold or Chiltern dining chairs or a cabinet on plinths.

Automatic washing machines were being mass-produced now – those who couldn't afford to buy one up-front could always pay "on the drip".

Domestic goddess, Fifties style

The new zebra crossing made shopping safer on Wavertree Road in 1952

Shopping is much more fun with a friend

Making the News 1957

CITY CELEBRATES 750 YEARS

The Queen Mother in the Speke garden of Mr and Mrs Hillman which was chosen to be inspected as part of her city walkabout

FOR Liverpool's 750th anniversary in the Charter fortnight of 1957 the city celebrated a visit from the Queen Mother.

On arrival at Lime Street in her special coach attached to the Red Rose express, she embarked on her elongated tour, visiting everywhere from the city library in William Brown Street and the Anglican Cathedral to the Dunlop factory – where she admired the quality of their tennis balls – and even popped in on a lucky couple's council house in Speke.

For the birthday fortnight, letters from Liverpool were franked with the message: "1207-1957 come to Liverpool for Liverpool Charter Celebrations from 16th to 30th June, 1957."

The Lord Mayor, Alderman Frank Cain, salutes the guard of honour at the Town Hall during the 1957 Charter celebrations

memorable movies!

NATIONAL HEADLINES

10 January: Harold Macmillan succeeds Anthony Eden as Prime Minister.

15 May: Britain drops its first H-bomb as part of a series of tests in the Pacific.

27 June: The link between smoking and lung cancer is one of 'direct cause and effect', a special report by the Medical Research Council finds. But tobacco firms rejected the findings saying they are merely a "matter of opinion."

1 October: A vaccine against the strain of influenza currently sweeping around the world is made available to the British public.

4 October: Russian satellite Sputnik is launched into space - the first man-made object ever to leave the Earth's atmosphere. In November Russia launches Laika the dog on Sputnik II.

25 December: The Royal Christmas Message is broadcast on television for the first time.

28 December: The Stanley Abattoir in Liverpool, the biggest abattoir in the north of England, is shut down after foot-and-mouth disease is found in cattle.

Top of the Pops:

- Lonnie Donegan – Cumberland Gap
- Elvis Presley – All Shook Up
- The Crickets – That'll Be The Day
- Paul Anka – Diana
- Harry Belafonte – Mary's Boy Child

Walking to training at Anfield – Billy Liddell front

Golden boots

True legends on and off the pitch

LIVERPOOL and Everton had some great soccer stars in the 1950s.

Liverpool all-time great Billy Liddell was held in such reverence by his adoring fans, they nicknamed the team Liddell-pool.

He dazzled with his ability and amazing skills. When he finally hung up his boots in 1960, he had completed 537 games for the club (495 League games) and scored a total of 229 goals.

Merseyside born Dave Hickson earned an eternal place in Everton folklore during the exciting run to the 1953 FA Cup semi-final, scoring vital goals, including a fifth round winner against Manchester United after leaving the field to have five stitches in a gashed eyebrow.

He notched 25 League goals during the 1953/54 promotion campaign but after one term in the top flight was sold to Aston Villa for £17,500. He returned to Everton at a bargain £7,500 in 1957 before moving across Stanley Park to Liverpool in 1959.

Sport

The spirit of the Fifties.
Dave Hickson, the 'Cannonball Kid'
in action at Goodison

Not the twin towers but the Tower Grounds, New Brighton. The 'Rakers' as New Brighton FC were known, take on Stockport in a Third Division North clash in 1950, the year before they dropped out of the Football League

Extra time

Still calling the shots

IN the days before multi-million pound footballers even the most talented and successful had to earn a living after retiring from the game.

If you popped into a grocers in West Kirby in the Fifties you may have been served by the legendary Joe Mercer, who had a number of shops on Wirral.

In Chester you could have your pint pulled at the Dublin Packet by the greatest goalscorer of them all William Ralph 'Dixie' Dean.

The amazing 1951 Grand National when only 3 horses actually finished, one of those was a remount. The race was won by Nickel Coin, the last mare to do so

National pride

Drama of the world's greatest race

THE Fifties was a fabulous decade for the Grand National.

The Liverpool specialist Freebooter survived a hair-raising error to triumph in 1950 when the French-bred Monaveen became the first Royal National contender for 42 years.

Vincent O'Brien, the legendary Irish trainer who retired in 1995, trained three consecutive 'National winners in Early Mist (1953), Royal Tan (1954) and Quare Times (1955).

This was just the start of his career, and he later went on to become arguably the greatest flat trainer ever seen with a record six Derbys among his successes.

The heartbreak of Devon Loch's collapse barely fifty yards from the post in 1956, brought both sympathy and admiration for the manner in which Her Majesty The Queen Mother put aside her disappointment in being the first to congratulate the winning connections.

Legendary Irish trainer Vincent O'Brien

Ferrari, Maserati and the great motor racing marques battle it out in the British Grand Prix

Below: Stirling Moss receives the victor's garland from Mrs Topham after his epic 1957 British Grand Prix victory

A racing cert

Aintree's life in the fast lane

GREAT stars of the track shone at Aintree in the 1950s in the glory days of motor racing.

Stirling Moss was a regular visitor, thrilling the crowd with his skill and daring deeds. Some of his most famous victories were scored at Aintree. In 1955, in the British Grand Prix, he had a terrific battle over the 300-mile course with world champion Juan Manuel Fangio, watched by a record crowd of 125,000. Moss, in his Mercedes Benz, recorded a dramatic inches victory over Fangio to become the first British driver to win the race.

From 1953, Aintree's impresario Mirabel Topham brought stars like Moss, Fangio, Hawthorn, Jack Brabham and Roy Salvadori and in 1955 attracted the biggest crowd ever to attend a motor sport fixture on any circuit in this country.

Above: Bootle take on Neston on a July Saturday in 1950

"Two, four, six, eight, who do we appreciate . . . C-H-A-D-S, CHADS". Harry Welch, captain of Liverpool Chads speedway team who raced at the Stanley track in Fairfield

The great Peter Craven in action for England. He graduated from riding for Liverpool Chads at the Stanley track in Fairfield, to becoming World Champion in 1955 and 1962

Billy Liddell, the heartbeat of Liverpool in the Fifties.
A true gentleman footballer

In 1950 you had to knit your own scarf, even more work if you wanted the names of the players on it. Expensive too as wool was still in short supply. Jimmy Seddon, Liverpool second team trainer is as engrossed in the action as the fans

The People's Champion. Nigerian-born Hogan 'Kid' Bassey arrives home to a Toxteth welcome after defending his World Featherweight title against Ricardo Moreno in 1958

Making the News
1958
A GAME OF TWO HALVES

DESPITE the Munich air disaster the previous February, England were by no means disgraced in their World Cup clash against Brazil in 1958, the first ever goalless game in the tournament's history.

England, once again led by the inspirational Billy Wright, put up a splendid performance against a teenage prodigy called Pelé, a devastating right-winger in Garrincha and Didi, an inside-forward of rare skill.

They managed to hold the eventual champions, chiefly thanks to some superb handling by Burnley goalkeeper Colin McDonald.

The 1958 World Cup in Gothenburg marked the debut on the world stage of 17-year-old Pelé, arguably the best player of all time.

With every touch of the ball, every pass, every dribble, the Brazilian was capable of coming up with something new.

A legend was born.

Above: Swedish goalkeeper Kalle Svensson struggles to contain rising star Pelé in the World Cup final

Left: The Munich Air crash was a tragic end for Busby's Babes

memorable movies!

NATIONAL HEADLINES

4 January: Sir Edmund Hillary reaches the South Pole - the first overland explorer to do so since Captain Robert F Scott's expedition in 1912.

6 February: The Munich air crash kills 21 passengers, including eight Manchester United players, eight journalists and five substitute members of the squad. It was a tragic end for "Busby's Babes", the most promising United squad for years.

29 April: The Broadway musical My Fair Lady opens for its first night in London, to a rapturous reception.

18 August: American actor Bonar Colleano is killed in a car crash in Birkenhead, shortly after exiting the Queensway Tunnel.

8 June: The sixth World Cup kicks off in Sweden. Brazil beat the hosts 5-2 in the final, marking the debut on the world stage of a 17-year-old Pelé.

21 December: General Charles de Gaulle is elected President of France with an overwhelming majority.

Top of the Pops:

- Jerry Lee Lewis – Great Balls Of Fire
- Everly Brothers – All I Have To Do Is Dream
- Connie Francis – Who's Sorry Now?
- Perry Como – Magic Moments
- Conway Twitty – It's Only Make Believe

If these walls could talk...

The changing faces of our streets and buildings

A quiet Bootle scene in 1952. One row of buildings, but two sets of addresses. Miller's Bridge houses had their entrances at the front. Those in Balliol Terrace which form the top row were reached from the rear

The inaugural BEA Liverpool - Cardiff helicopter service in May 1950 comes in to land at Speke's art deco terminal

A sooty Liver Building forms the backdrop to the Irish Sea ferries in Princes Dock in 1958

Like abandoned gateways to the past, the last two supporting arches of the recently demolished Overhead Railway stand sentinel on their own island in the Strand. Behind lies Tower Building, designed by W Aubrey Thomas, architect of the Royal Liver Building, and St Nicholas Church

The scars of war are still evident on the junction of Lord Street and Paradise Street. The Blitz site is put to good use by the Conservatives for some tailboard electioneering during the 1951 general election campaign

Bright lights, big city. The famous Guinness Clock and the neon signs of St George's Crescent illuminate the 1959 traffic along Lime Street. Pictured right, St John's Lane

Below: This looks like the high street of a rural English county town, but it is Lark Lane in 1951

An impressive picture of the multi-storey flats rising above the city on the Everton Heights, 1959

Water Street 1955, looking towards Dale Street. A number 6 tram makes its way towards the Pier head

The six o'clock scene at the Liverpool entrance to the Mersey Tunnel, August 10, 1954

Traffic at 9.15am edges along from Wellington Column,
towards the Queensway Tunnel entrance – August 12, 1955

Night-time conditions on a January lunchtime in 1959. Shoppers on the zebra crossing at the junction of Parker Street and Church Street

Smog city

Through darker days

THEY were almost comforting, those dense fogs that engulfed the winter streets.

The stillness as the traffic crawled on, headlights blazing through the gloom, cars struggling to get round corners.

The darkness invaded our world and as a young child it could be quite terrifying, barely being able to see your hand in front of your face, let alone the pavement or the other side of the road.

It really was as thick as pea soup.

There may have been a certain ghostly romance in the fog, but it was a killer, particularly when it mixed with the pollutants belching from the factories to become a smog, destroying the lungs of men and women, many of whom were heavy smokers.

To combat smog, 6-and-a-half pence (3p) mouth masks could be bought from the chemists.

Marooned in a sea of swirling grey cloud, a policewoman directs the sparse traffic on Church Street

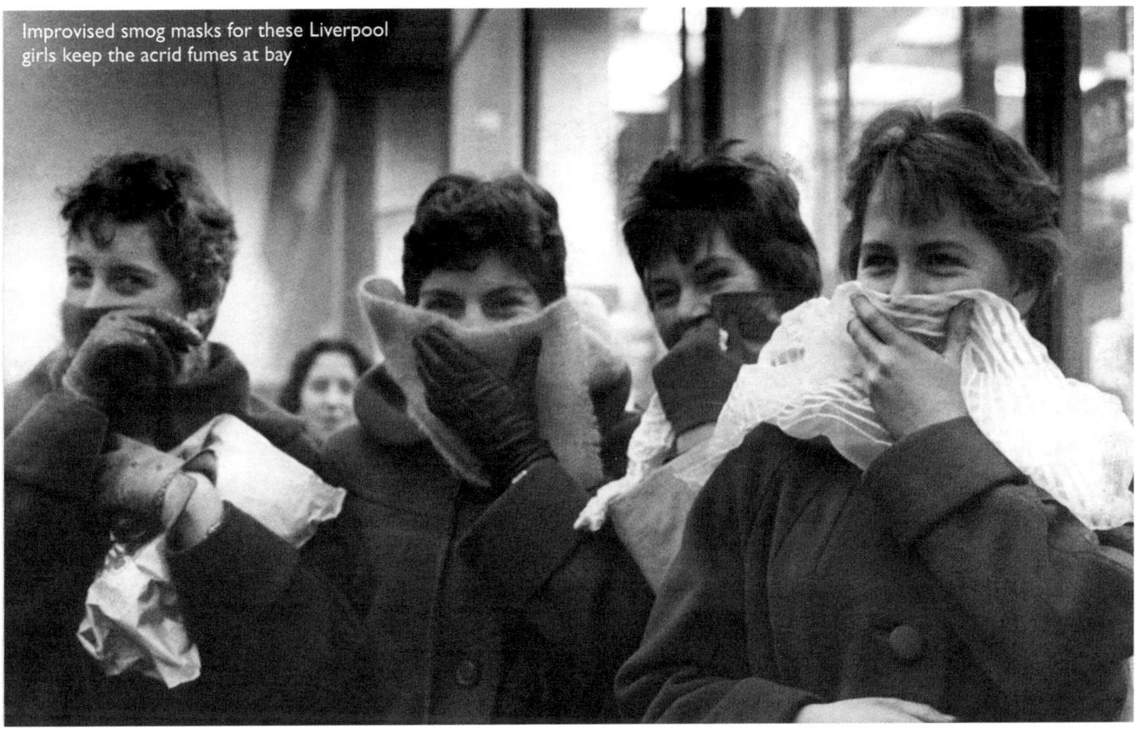

Improvised smog masks for these Liverpool girls keep the acrid fumes at bay

NATIONAL HEADLINES

3 February: Buddy Holly's plane crashes in Clear Lake, Iowa, ending the career of a musical genius.

16 February: Cuba's revolutionary leader Fidel Castro is sworn in as Prime Minister in Havana.

24 May: Empire Day is renamed Commonwealth Day.

28 May: Monkeys Able and Baker are launched 300 miles into space from Cape Canaveral, Florida. They become the first living creatures to survive a space flight.

26 August: The first MINI goes in sale.

5 September: The UK's first trunk dialling system from a public call-box is inaugurated in Bristol. It is the start of a countrywide service that will eventually replace the Button A and Button B pre-payment system.

9 October: Harold 'Supermac' Macmillan leads the Conservatives to general election victory for a third successive term.

26 October: The world sees pictures of the far side of the moon for the first time, from the Soviet satellite Lunik 3.

Top of the Pops:

- Russ Conway – Roulette
- Bobby Darin – Dream Lover
- Adam Faith – What Do You Want
- Cliff Richard And The Drifters – Livin Doll
- Emile Ford And The Checkmates – What Do You Want To Make Those Eyes At Me For

Making the News
1959
THE DAY THE MUSIC DIED

Rock and roll legend: Buddy Holly had a resounding influence on Liverpool's young musicians of the day

ON February 3, 1959, Buddy Holly's plane crashed in Iowa, killing the 22-year-old star as well as Richie Valens and The Big Bopper.

The loss was felt around the world and in Liverpool the mourning for Buddy Holly was almost as great as in his hometown of Lubbock.

The bespectacled musician and his Crickets played two concerts at the Philharmonic Hall on March 20, 1958 – at 6.15pm and 8.30pm. They were dates that Liverpool fans would never forget.

The career of American pop star Richie Valens was tragically short. In May 1958 he had his first hit Come On, Let's Go. When they buried Valens, his second record Donna was reaching number two in the American charts to become a posthumous best seller.

Jiles Perry Richardson Junior, or The Big Bopper, is best known for his recording of Chantilly Lace.

February 3, 1959, was to become known through Don McLean's American Pie, as "the day the music died."

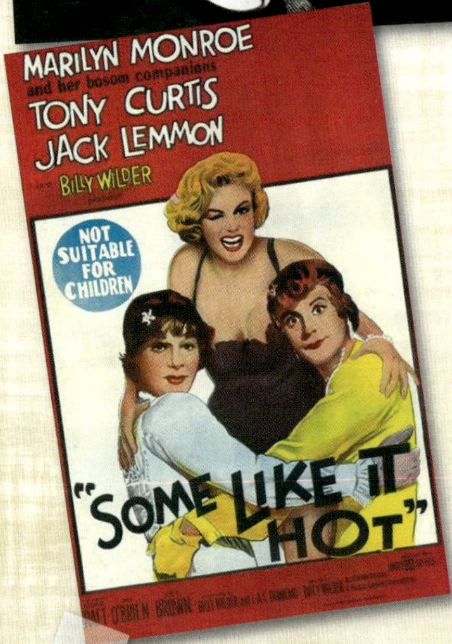

Big ambitions for the MINI

Children keep their cool in the Steble Fountain at
William Brown Street, on the hottest day in August, 1953

Other publications from

Trinity Mirror NW²

Discover Liverpool
£12.50+
Free P+P UK only
Save £7.50

Echoes of Liverpool
£4.50+
Free P+P UK only

Liverpool Life
£3.99+
£1.50 P+P UK only

Mersey Maritime Tales
£3.99+
£1.50 P+P UK only

Mersey Mastermind
£8.99+
Free P+P UK only

The Great Liverpool Pub Crawl
£8.99+
Free P+P UK only

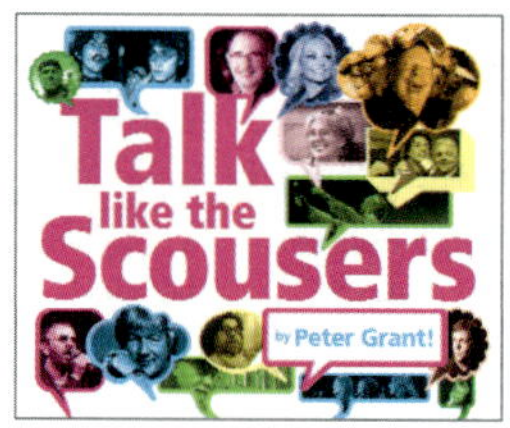

Talk like the Scousers
£8.99+
Free P+P UK only

Dummy Bullets
£6.99+
Free P+P UK only

Visit www.merseyshop.com or call 0845 143 0001
Monday to Friday 9am-5pm

Trinity Mirror NW²

Trinity Mirror North West & North Wales
PO Box 48, Old Hall Street, Liverpool L69 3EB

Trinity Mirror Sports Media Executive Editor
Ken Rogers